What Is Your Mom Doing?

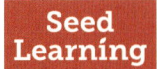
Seed Learning

What is your mom doing?

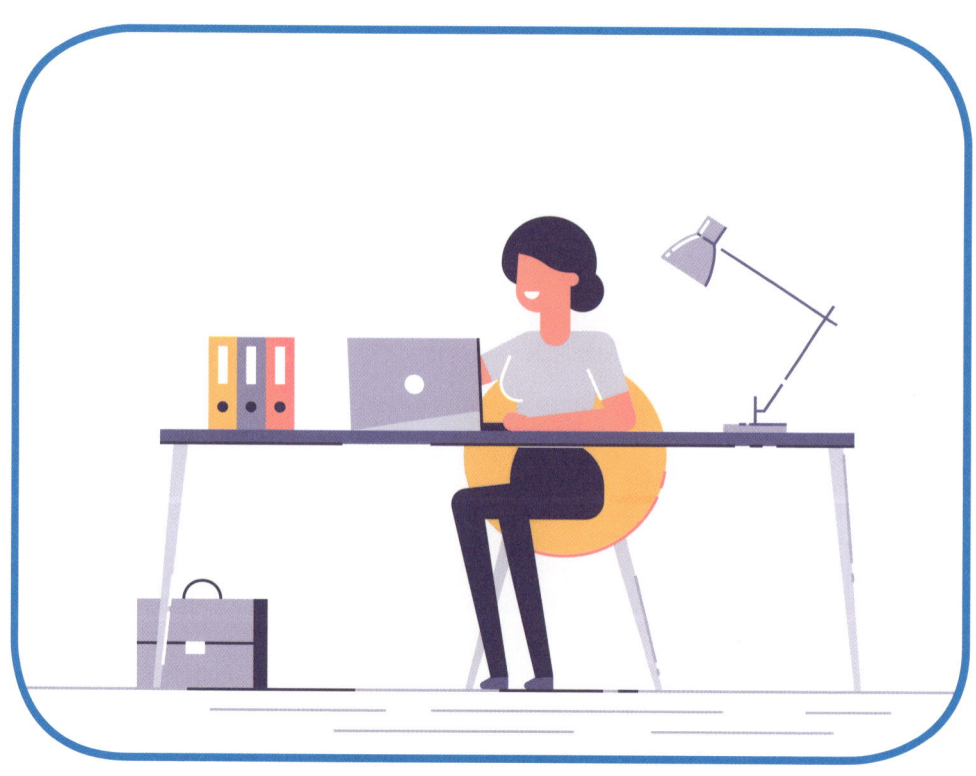

Working.

My mom is working.

What is your dad doing?

Fishing.

My dad is
fishing.

What is your sister doing?

Singing.

My sister is
singing.

What is your brother doing?

Running.

My brother is running.

What is your grandma doing?

Baking.

My grandma is baking.

What is your grandpa doing?

Reading.

My grandpa is
reading.

What is your friend doing?

Studying.

My friend is studying.

Let's learn about Hajj.

July

Sunday	Monday	Tuesday	Wednesday	Thursday	Friday	Saturday
			1	2	3	4
5	6	(7)	8	9	10	11
12	13	14	15	16	17	18
19	20	21	22	23	24	25
26	27	28	29	30	31	

Trace the word July and circle the date.